First World War
and Army of Occupation
War Diary
France, Belgium and Germany

51 DIVISION
Divisional Troops
D Squadron North Irish Horse
1 May 1915 - 1 April 1916

WO95/2854/1

The Naval & Military Press Ltd
www.nmarchive.com
Published in association with The National Archives

Published by

The Naval & Military Press Ltd

Unit 10 Ridgewood Industrial Park,

Uckfield, East Sussex,

TN22 5QE England

Tel: +44 (0) 1825 749494

www.naval-military-press.com

www.nmarchive.com

This diary has been reprinted in facsimile from the original. Any imperfections are inevitably reproduced and the quality may fall short of modern type and cartographic standards.

© **Crown Copyright**
Images reproduced by permission of The National Archives, London, England, 2015.

Contents

Document type	Place/Title	Date From	Date To
Heading	WO95/2854/1 D Sqdn Nth Irish Horse 1915 May-1916 April		
Heading	51st Division 'D' Sqdn Nth Irish Horse May 1915-Apr 1916. To 7 Corps		
Heading	D Sqn. N. Ir. Horse May-Dec 1915 Vol I		
Heading	War Diary of D Sqn North Irish Horse From May 1st 1915 to Dec 31st 1915 (Volume 1A)		
War Diary	Southampton	01/05/1915	01/05/1915
War Diary	Havre	02/05/1915	02/05/1915
War Diary	Busnes	03/05/1915	05/05/1915
War Diary	Pradelles	14/05/1915	14/05/1915
War Diary	La Gorgue	19/05/1915	19/05/1915
War Diary	Hinges	20/05/1915	20/05/1915
War Diary	Carvin	01/06/1915	01/06/1915
War Diary	Le Touret	14/06/1915	14/06/1915
War Diary	Le Pacault	21/06/1915	21/06/1915
War Diary	Neuf Berquin	25/06/1915	25/06/1915
War Diary	Heilly	28/07/1915	28/07/1915
War Diary	Franvillers	05/08/1915	05/08/1915
War Diary	Behencourt	14/08/1915	14/08/1915
War Diary	Septenville	26/12/1915	26/12/1915
War Diary	Southampton	01/05/1915	01/05/1915
War Diary	Havre	01/05/1915	01/05/1915
War Diary	Berguette	03/05/1915	04/05/1915
War Diary	Busnes	04/05/1915	04/05/1915
War Diary	Pradelles	14/05/1915	14/05/1915
War Diary	La Gorgue	19/05/1915	19/05/1915
War Diary	Hinges	20/05/1915	21/05/1915
War Diary	Carvin	01/06/1915	01/06/1915
War Diary	Le Touret	14/06/1915	14/06/1915
War Diary	Carvin	18/06/1915	18/06/1915
War Diary	La Pannerie	21/06/1915	21/06/1915
War Diary	Neuf Berquin	27/06/1915	01/07/1915
War Diary	Berguette	27/07/1915	27/07/1915
War Diary	Mericourt	28/07/1915	28/07/1915
War Diary	Heilly	28/07/1915	28/07/1915
War Diary	Martinsart	29/07/1915	29/07/1915
War Diary	Authville	30/07/1915	30/07/1915
War Diary	Heilly Authville Trenches	01/08/1915	01/08/1915
War Diary	Franvillers	05/08/1915	05/08/1915
War Diary	Behencourt	13/08/1915	13/08/1915
War Diary	Behencourt	09/09/1915	12/12/1915
War Diary	Septenville	26/12/1915	26/12/1915
Heading	War Diary of D Sqn-North Irish Horse From Jan 1st 1916 to Jan 31st 1916 (Volume 2)		
War Diary	Septenville	01/01/1916	01/01/1916
Heading	D Sqn Irish Horse Feb Vol III		
War Diary	Septenville	01/02/1916	01/02/1916
War Diary	Corbie	08/02/1916	08/02/1916
War Diary	Flesselles	29/02/1916	29/02/1916

Heading	War Diary of "D" Sqn North Irish Horse. From March 1st 1916 to March 31st 1916 (Volume IV)		
War Diary	Flesselles	01/02/1916	01/02/1916
War Diary	Hardinval	06/03/1916	06/03/1916
War Diary	Sericourt	09/03/1916	09/03/1916
War Diary	Berlencourt	12/03/1916	12/03/1916
War Diary	Tilloy-Les-Hemaville	14/03/1916	14/03/1916
War Diary	Vandelicourt	15/03/1916	15/03/1916
Heading	War Diary of D Sqn North Irish Horse From April 1st 1916 to April 30th 1916 (Volume V)		
War Diary	Vandelicourt	01/04/1916	01/04/1916

WO 95 2854/1

D Sqdn. 12th Irish Horse
1915 May - 1916 April

51ST DIVISION

'D' SQDN NTH IRISH HORSE

MAY 1915-APR 1916.

To 7 Corps

"D" Sqt. N. Ini Home
May — Dec 1915
Vol. 1

Army Form C. 2118.

31

WAR DIARY
or
INTELLIGENCE SUMMARY.

CONFIDENTIAL

War Diary

of

D Sqdn North IRISH HORSE

from MAY 1st 1915 to Dec. 31st 1915

(Volume 1A)

Army Form C. 2118.

WAR DIARY
or
INTELLIGENCE SUMMARY.
(Erase heading not required.)

Instructions regarding War Diaries and Intelligence Summaries are contained in F. S. Regs., Part II. and the Staff Manual respectively. Title pages will be prepared in manuscript.

Place	Date	Hour	Summary of Events and Information	Remarks and references to Appendices
			51st (Highland) Division	
SOUTHAMPTON	1.5.15	6 A.M.	"X" Sq" North Irish Horse left COPLE (BEDFORD) on 30-4-15 under Major Hon G.A. Hamilton-Russell arrived at SOUTHAMPTON at 6 A.M. 1-5-15. Embarked at	
HAVRE	2.5.15	6 A.M.	SOUTHAMPTON at 4 P.M. in two transports and arrived at HAVRE at 6 A.M. 2-5-15. — Entrained at 10 P.M. 2-5-15 and arrived at BERGUETTE at	
BUSNES	3rd/4th 5/15	12 midnight	12 midnight 3/4-5-15. Proceeded at once to BUSNES. The Squadron consists of the following officers:— Major Hon G.A. HAMILTON-RUSSELL. MAJOR HOLT WARING. 2nd Lt J.G.Q. KIRKPATRICK. 2nd Lt W. MURLAND. 2nd Lt J.V. ADAIR. 2nd Lt C. WISE. 141 N.C.O's & Men. 158 Riding & Draught Horses. 2nd Lt J. MARTIN joined the Squadron on disembarkation at HAVRE on 2-5-15. At BUSNES the 51st Division remained in Reserve Billets under G.H.Q. on	
PRADELLES	14.5.15	1 P.M.	14-5-15. 1st Division moved note via HAZEBROUCK to PRADELLES & came under 1st Command North Indian Army Corps (Lt Gen Sir J. Wilcocks Commanding) —	
LA GORGUE	19.5.15	11 A.M.	On 19-5-15 the Division moved to LA GORGUE & on this day Major Holt-WARING left "D" Sq" N.I.H. & went to BAILLEUL to take command of "C" Sq" North Irish Horse. Capt E King being transferred to same Sq" from "C" Sq" to "D" Sq". On 20-5-15 the Division moved South & H.Q.	

Army Form C. 2118.

WAR DIARY
or
INTELLIGENCE SUMMARY.

(Erase heading not required.)

Instructions regarding War Diaries and Intelligence Summaries are contained in F. S. Regs., Part II. and the Staff Manual respectively. Title pages will be prepared in manuscript.

Place	Date	Hour	Summary of Events and Information	Remarks and references to Appendices
HINGES	20.5.15	2 P.M.	S.H.A. being at LOCON. D Sq. M.M. at HINGES (North of LA BASSÉE CANAL) - on	
	1-6-15		The Division joins 4th Army Corps (Lt. Gen. Sir H. RAWLINSON) on the	
CARVIN	1-6-15	3 P.M.	Regt (less Sq.) moved to CARVIN (near ROBEC) remaining there until	
	21-6-15		During the period 14/17 there was a big British attack at FESTUBERT	
LE TOURET	14.6.15	5 P.M.	and our troops were employed to form a prisoner's escort at LE TOURET.	
LE PACAULT	21.6.15	11 AM	The Sq² moved on the 21-6-15 to LE PACAULT & thence on the 25-6-15 to	
NEUF BER- GUIN	25-6-15	1 P.M.	NEUF BERGUIN (near BETHUNE (RES)) & were under command 7th Indian Army Corps. - 30-6-15 Capt E. King King Edward's Hospital & was subsequently invalided to England. From the 21st June to 28 July - K.Sq & Supply Branch rehearsing & practising Night parties by day & by night. At 10 P.M. 27-7-15 The Sq. marched to BERGUETTE Stⁿ & entrained - proceeded via CALAIS & ABBEVILLE to MERICOURT Stⁿ arriving there 6 P.M. 28-7-15	
HEILLY	28-7-15	7 P.M.	Marched to HEILLY. On the 29-7-15. 3 officers & 60 men of K. Sq² were attached to the 152 Bde (Brigadier Genⁿ Ross) & marched to MARTINSART - took over trenches from the French on the 30-7-15 at AUTHUILLE. On the	
FRANVILLERS	5-8-15	1 P.M.	5-8-15. The remainder of the Sq² with led horses moved to FRANVILLERS,	

WAR DIARY
or
INTELLIGENCE SUMMARY

Army Form C. 2118.

Place	Date	Hour	Summary of Events and Information	Remarks and references to Appendices
			115 men of 8th W.D.B. & Lt Sqn being attacks which on the trenches to be 1/8 Argyll & Suther- land Highlanders. On the 13-8-15 the Sqn was retired to the trenches by a Sqn of 3 B.C. Lancers (Skinner's Horse) & being met at Albert on	
Behencourt	14-8-15	4 a.m.	10 PM by led horses marches to Behencourt arriving her 4 a.m. 14-8-15. One man was slightly wounded in the shoulder during the period in the trenches.	
	16-8-15		P.D. Sherston joins the Sqn from Antrim.	
	24-8-15		2 Lts P.D. Bannatine Allason over Command of the 1st W Div. & Major Sir E.C.M. Harper R.C.B. D.S.O. — which or Behencourt the Sqn supplies orderlies & hear repair parties, & daily working parties. Built winter stable, & made Comportable winter quarters.	
Septen- ville	26.12.15	1 PM	On the 26-12-15 the Sqn left Behencourt & marches to Septenville. The 51st Div'n being withdrawn from the line & retires to rest in a back area. — 4-1-16 The Div'n joins the XIII Corps.	

Alan the ...
O.C. ... L. Sqn 2-15
... L.M. 15... 2-15

Army Form C. 2118.

May (1)

WAR DIARY or INTELLIGENCE SUMMARY.
(Erase heading not required.)

Place	Date	Hour	Summary of Events and Information	Remarks and references to Appendices
SOUTHAMPTON	1-5-15	3 A.M.	One half the men of B Sqn. North Irish Horse, together with all Sqn. Horses & Major Hugh A. HAMILTON, RUSSELL, 2/Lt. L.G.C. KIRKPATRICK and 2/Lt. W. MURLAND on board the ANGLO-CANADIAN left SOUTHAMPTON at 6 P.M. & arrived at HAVRE at 11 A.M. 2-5-15. The remaining men of HQ Sqn. under Major HOLT HARING, 2/Lt. HAYADAR & 2/Lt. LOWISE on board the EMPRESS QUEEN left HAVRE at 7 P.M. 1-5-15 and arrived at HAVRE at 9 a.m. 2-5-15. - Men & horses	
HAVRE				
BERGUETTE	2-5-15	midnight 12 a.m.	disembarked at once & rested at the dock during the day. at 10 P.M. 2-5-15 HQ Sqn & Subalterns of	
BUSNES	4-5-15	5 a.m.	HAVRE station leaving at 1 a.m. for BERGUETTE - arriving there at 12 midnight 3/4-5-15 and detrained in heavy rain. BUSNES was reached at 5 a.m. 4-5-15 and the men billetted in Barns. the Sqn. horses being placed in 2 orchards - the Division (51st) being shortly under the orders of G.H.Q. on the 9-5-15 a very violent attack was begun by the British in the neighbourhood of FESTUBERT - the Indian army Corps being engaged. This engagement lasted 4 days but no great success was obtained. - The Road from BERGUETTE to BUSNES was good.	
PRADELLES	14-5-15	3 P.M.	The Division marched north on the 14-5-15. The Sqn. marched at 9 a.m. via H. VENANT - HAZEBROUK to PRADELLES, the Division now coming under the orders of the G.O.C. Indian Army Corps. (Sir J. Willcocks) - The Road was in good order. Men were billetted in 3 Barns & the horse lines in an open grass field. ample for horse exercise in a level field. Drinking water from local trumps. Ref. map 1/40,000 BETHUNE	

May (1)

Army Form C. 2118.

WAR DIARY
or
INTELLIGENCE SUMMARY.
(Erase heading not required.)

Place	Date	Hour	Summary of Events and Information	Remarks and references to Appendices
LA GORGUE	19.5.15	11 a.m.	at 8.a.m 19-5-15 the Sq" marches to LA GORGUE (via VIEUX BERQUIN) the roads somewhat cut up under traffic — the Sq" bivouacks near a pontoon factory south of LA GORGUE - MERVILLE Road). MAJOR HOLT WARING left (C Sq" During) his march & proceeds to take over "C Sq" North Irish Horse attached to 3rd Div" in the neighbourhood of BAILLEUL. Capt E KING KING handovers from C Sq" North Irish Horse joining D Sq" this day from C Sq".	
HINGES	20.5.15	at 10 a.m. 20-5-15 the Sq" marches via PARADIS to farm north of LA BASSÉE CANAL — 1 mile N of HINGES — the road was being a 2nd Class road — in fair order, arrives at billets 3 P.m. the men billetted in a barn, horses in an open Grass Field.	Ref. map 1/40000 BETHUNE
	21.5.15		The 2nd & 4th Div"s were relieved by the Highland (51st) & Canadian Div"s — the Div" moved in to the 4 Army Corps Command (GER. Sir J. Rawlinson). The 15th remained to hut N of HINGES until the 1-6-15 when it marches to CARVIN. During the month the weather generally fine & warm. There were occasional showers but not sufficient to damage the roads to any great extent.	

June (1)

WAR DIARY
or
INTELLIGENCE SUMMARY.
(Erase heading not required.)

Army Form C. 2118.

Instructions regarding War Diaries and Intelligence Summaries are contained in F. S. Regs., Part II. and the Staff Manual respectively. Title pages will be prepared in manuscript.

Place	Date	Hour	Summary of Events and Information	Remarks and references to Appendices
CARVIN	1-6-15	5 P.M.	The Squadron marched at 2.30 P.M. 1-6-15 to CARVIN. Arrived at 5 P.M. - Route taken partially along canal bank. - Horses dry & in good order. The Squadron lines were situated in a shady orchard, good water obtained from small stream. The men in barns. On this day the Prime Minister inspected through & heavy the 51st Divisional area & addressed the troops.	
LE TOURET	14-6-15 6 P.M.		Two troops under Capt. E. KING. KING moved via LOCON to LE TOURET - bivouacking in the neighbourhood of the farm to act as prisoners escort. These two troops were relieved on the 16th by Hussars, 2 troops under Major Hon. A. HAMILTON RUSSELL on 16-6-15. These troops returned to CARVIN on 18-6-15. No prisoners were handed over to O.C. Sqn during these 4 days.	
CARVIN	18-6-15			
LA PANNERIE	21-6-15	2 P.M.	Sqn marches via BOIS du PACAULT to LA PANNERIE at 10 a.m. Horse lines situated in open grass field W. of village - Men in a barn. - Roads dry & in good order. H.Div? on the 24-6-15. certain units of the Division started to move to ESTAIRES & came into the command of LA GORGUE.	
NEUF BERQUIN	27-6-15	2.30 P.M.	The Indian army corps. at 9 a.m. 27-6-15 the Sqn moved northwest to ESTAIRES to NEUF BERQUIN arriving 2.30 P.M. A heavy thunderstorm fell during the march. - The roads were in good order. Horse lines in an orchard, on the bank of the NEUF BERQUIN - ESTAIRE Road. - Horses were watered in the canal at LA GORGUE - Drinking water was scarce, obtainable in small quantities from Pumps in Neuf Berquin.	Ref map 40000 BETHUNE

Army Form C. 2118.

WAR DIARY
or
INTELLIGENCE SUMMARY.
(Erase heading not required.)

June (2)

Place	Date	Hour	Summary of Events and Information	Remarks and references to Appendices
			The weather during June (1 – 25) was extremely hot & dry. No rain falling. On the 25th a severe thunderstorm followed by others on the 26th & 27th broke the weather. On the 30.6.14 Capt E. KING KING left for the base to attend a medical board. He was suffering from debility & overstrain, in order to go to ENGLAND.	

Army Form C. 2118.

WAR DIARY
or
INTELLIGENCE SUMMARY.
(Erase heading not required.)

Instructions regarding War Diaries and Intelligence Summaries are contained in F. S. Regs., Part II. and the Staff Manual respectively. Title pages will be prepared in manuscript.

July.

Place	Date	Hour	Summary of Events and Information	Remarks and references to Appendices
NEUF BERQUIN	1/7/15		Working parties of up to 100 men in the Support trenches & for the construction of trenches to carry a subterranean telephone wire from D.H.Q. to the Bde H.Q's in case of an enemy attack were found by the J.S.'s on the 3-6. 9-10. 12-13. 14-15. 16-17. 18-19. 20. & 21. of the month. — This work was on the 2 mile East of LAVENTIE. 2/Lt W. MURLAND & 2/Lt A.V. ADAIR & 4 N.C.O.'s were instructed in "Bombing" with a bombing school (154th Bde) at LAVENTIE from 16-7-15 to 23-7-15.	
BERGUETTE	27.7.15 11 PM		The J.S.'s marches at 9.30 PM via MERVILLE to BERGUETTE and entrained, proceeding	
MERICOURT	28.7.15 6 PM		via BOULOGNE - ABBEVILLE & AMIENS to MEAULTE MERICOURT St?. detrained	
HEILLY	28/7/15 7 PM		at 6.0.p.m. & marches to HEILLY arriving at 7 PM. 28.7.15. RUSSELL	
MARTINSART	29.7.15 10.30 PM		Major A. HAMILTON. 2/Lt N.J.G.C. KIRKPATRICK, J.V. ADAIR & 60 men were attached to the 152" Bde & marches at 7 PM via ALBERT to MARTINSART. The remaining men of the S.S. & horses remained at HEILLY under 2/Lt W. MURLAND.	
AUTHUILLE	30.7.15 6.15 a.m.		Major HAMILTON RUSSELL - two officers & 60. O.R. proceeded at 10 P.M & marches to the Trenches at AUTHUILLE - were attached to the 1/8 ARGYLL & SUTHERLAND HIGHLANDERS (Lt.Col CAMPBELL comdg). These trenches were taken over then major from the 116th French Regiment.	

REF MAP BETHUNE / 40,000
REF MAP AMIENS / 100,000

WAR DIARY or INTELLIGENCE SUMMARY

Army Form C. 2118.

Place	Date	Hour	Summary of Events and Information	Remarks and references to Appendices
HEILLY / AUTHUILLE TRENCHES	1-8-15		The Sqd'n horses remained at HEILLY, on lv 5-8-15 they moved to FRANVILLERS. The Sqd'n officers & 60 O.R. in the trenches, near AUTHUILLE came out of the trenches at 8 P.M. 13-8-15 being relieved by 3rd LANCERS (SKINNER'S HORSE). — During their period in the trenches (30-7-15 to 13-8-15) their casualties were one slightly wounded by a dropping bullet. This man, Pte. McGIVERN, & SS. Cook being in a RESERVE trench.	
FRANVILLERS	5-8-15		During this period there was a considerable amount of rifle fire especially early morning & evening, & some shelling by both artilleries of reserve trenches, the fire trenches not being shelled at all, — no trench mortars or bombs thrown by enemy. The 111th Reserve Regt. was said to be in trenches of the enemy opposite to our own. The trenches on lv night – (tonight?) of THIEPVAL CHATEAU were shelled by our artillery. At 1.30 a.m. 14-8-15 we took our horses at R4.BR.W of ALBERT & marched to BEHENCOURT, rejoining the remainder of the Sqd'n which has moved from FRANVILLERS to BEHENCOURT on lv 13-8-15.	
BEHENCOURT	13-8-15		24-8-15. MAJOR GEN'L BANNATYNE-ALLASON C.B. handed over 51st Div. to MAJOR GEN'L G.M. HARPUR C.B. D.S.O. & returning to England & took of the 61st Div? On lv 27-28-29-30-31 Aug. the Sqd'n furnishing digging parties of 1 Off. 50 O.R's for construction of trenches weir of ALBERT. REF. MAP. ALBERT 1/40.000	

WAR DIARY or INTELLIGENCE SUMMARY

Army Form C. 2118.

Place: BEHENCOURT
Date: 9/15

Summary of Events and Information:

The SS's found a working party of 50 men for the trenches on the 1-9-15. on the 8-9-15. 2/Lt P. SMERSTON No.4.H. joined the 15th from ANTRIM.

During this month the men (N.C.O.s) were given instruction in map reading – riding school – a weekly scheme. from the 23-9-15 to 30-9-15 a party of 30 men was detailed daily for work cutting & supplying wood required in the trenches on 24-9-15 Major Gen'l BANNATYNE-ALLASON C.B. handed over to 51st Div & Major Gen'l Sir C.H. HARPUR C.B. D.S.O. returned to ENGLAND & took over 61st Div.

on the 25-9-15- The Big attack by the British troops at LOOS & the French at CHAMPAGNE began, which ended in some progress being made by both the BRITISH & FRENCH, a few miles of ground recovered from the enemy.

The weather was fine & warm during this month – some wet & cold weather for the 25th to the 30th itself.

Remarks and references to Appendices

WAR DIARY or INTELLIGENCE SUMMARY

Army Form C. 2118.

Place	Date	Hour	Summary of Events and Information	Remarks and references to Appendices
BEHENCOURT	10/15		5-10-15. A draught of 1 Sergt. & 8 O.R. arrived from le Havre & joined the Squadron.	
			11.10.15. A draught of 1 Cpl. & 9 O.R. arrived from le Havre, joined the Squadron, being in the Squadron at Montruplet.	
			7.10.15. The Sq.n horses were moved from the lines into stables in the village.	
			9.10.15. Dr SS inspected by G.O.C. 5th Div.n	
			23-10-15. King GEORGE - President POINCARÉ reviewed the troops Div. & lt Corps (5 - 30 - 5¼) Div.n) a few miles west of ALBERT.	
			Working parties in the trenches near AVELUY on 20-10-15 under 2Lt P SMERSTON & in the 30-10-15 under Lt KIRKPATRICK.	
			During the month of October - LtQs formed a daily working party of 30 N.C.O.s & men. Has also built stables - Bath house - Officers latrines - wash house - repaired barns - made beds - & established a Canteen & Institute in the village.	
			Fine weather the greater part of the month.	

WAR DIARY
or
INTELLIGENCE SUMMARY.

Army Form C. 2118.

Place	Date	Hour	Summary of Events and Information	Remarks and references to Appendices
BEHENCOURT	1/15		During November the daily work taken fatigue party of 30 N.C.O's & men was continued. Work in BEHENCOURT in connection with stabling & making the village comfortable for troops to winter in, was continued. About 700 French troops the 292nd & 326th Regts under Col. BROUOT arrived in BETHENCOURT on the 9th. — on the 16.11.16 - Major Gen. HARPER CB inspected the horses & instituted the 4th. Some snow fell on the 17.11.15 - melted on the 20.11.15 -. There was a hard frost - cold weather - on the 25th 26th 27th 28th 29th 30th.	

WAR DIARY
or
INTELLIGENCE SUMMARY.
(Erase heading not required.)

Army Form C. 2118.

Place	Date	Hour	Summary of Events and Information	Remarks and references to Appendices
BEHENCOURT	12/15		During December (1-20) - 30 N.C.O's + men went employs in hospitals daily.	
SEPTENVILLE	26/1/15		On the 26.12.15 - The squadron marched via MOLLIENS-AU-BOIS to SEPTENVILLE. a 2nd Class Road in fair condition. Training - Schemes - Drill + musketry were carried out during this month. a Sq. 2 Sous Just Horse (Major STERN i/c Command) attached the XXXII Div. succeeded the 88th at BEHENCOURT + took over the stables, billets, beds - canteen etc which he Sq. had made. SEPTENVILLE a small village 1 mil S of RUREMPRE consisting of 2 farms + a shooting lodge. nothing has been prepared by troops previously billetted there for the comfort of troops during the winter months. Weather during December was on a whole mild - fine.	REF Map AMIENS 1/100,000

Army Form C. 2118.

WAR DIARY
or
INTELLIGENCE SUMMARY.
(Erase heading not required.)

51/3

CONFIDENTIAL

WAR DIARY
of
NORTH IRISH HORSE

From ~~July 1st 1915~~
D Sqn Jan 1st 1916
to Jan 31st 1916

(VOLUME 2)

Army Form C. 2118.

WAR DIARY
or
INTELLIGENCE SUMMARY.
(Erase heading not required.)

Instructions regarding War Diaries and Intelligence Summaries are contained in F. S. Regs., Part II. and the Staff Manual respectively. Title pages will be prepared in manuscript.

Jan/16

Place	Date	Hour	Summary of Events and Information	Remarks and references to Appendices
SEPTENVILLE	1/1/16		During Jan'y 1916 the 15th war stations at SEPTENVILLE and continued their training whilst the Division remained in reserve. On the 12/1/16 the Divisional area was inspected by the C-in-C & G.O.C. 3rd Army. The Division during the month came under Command of the XIII Corps, and Lt. Gen: CONGREVE. V.C. The 15th was employed in making road reconnaissance reports of the Divisional area. The weather was fine on the whole - mild for the time of year.	

1577 Wt.W10791/1773 500,000 1/15 D. D. & L. A.D.S.S./Forms/C. 2118.

51

D Sqn N Irish Horse
Feb
Vol XIII

WAR DIARY or INTELLIGENCE SUMMARY

Army Form C. 2118.

Place	Date	Hour	Summary of Events and Information	Remarks and references to Appendices
SEPTENVILLE	1-2-16		The Squadron with Train Horses were quartered at SEPTENVILLE in the Commune de RUBEMPRÉ from the 26.12.15 to the 8-2-16. The horses belong to 1, 2, & 3 troops were under the shelter of out-houses – No. 4 troop in the open in an orchard. The men were billeted in barns. Water drawn from a well 250 ft deep. Was good for men & horses.	
CORBIE	8-2-16		The Sq'n under orders of G.O.C. 152nd Bde marches via HOLLIENS-au-BOIS & SEPRATFY QUERRIEU to CORBIE. The 8th & 9th Br's still remains in Reserve. – 2.40 or 3 hours. The Squadron was billeted in RUE VICTOR HUGO – CORBIE. The men in 3 Sheds at the SOIR Sud & higher, the horses in the open on the bank of a narrow running parallel to the SOMME RIVER & CANAL – the conditions were unfavorable for horses. & the horses were sent to Bde. Snow fell & the depth of 4" on the 23/24 Feb 1916. My middle on the 25 + 26. The Br then the men in Barns with the Squadron HQ & T.M.S.G. Corps.	
FLESSELLES	29.2.16		The Sq'n marches at 8.15 on the Vic BAOURS – AMIENS to FLESSELLES. The march of the Division on this occasion being contested by groups – each group under a commander – 16 SS M.M + Cyclists to form one Group. FLESSELLES was reached on 2 PM weather fine. Road good – The men were billeted in the RUE d'AMIENS in barns – horses in orchard near the road – water was obtained from a well in the neighbourhood of RUE d'AMIENS.	

Army Form C. 2118.

51

WAR DIARY
or
INTELLIGENCE SUMMARY.

CONFIDENTIAL

WAR DIARY
of
"D" Sqⁿ North Irish Horse.

From March 1ˢᵗ 1916   to March 31ˢᵗ 1916

(Volume ~~III~~ IV)

WAR DIARY or INTELLIGENCE SUMMARY.

Army Form C. 2118.

(Erase heading not required.)

Instructions regarding War Diaries and Intelligence Summaries are contained in F.S. Regs., Part II. and the Staff Manual respectively. Title pages will be prepared in manuscript.

Place	Date	Hour	Summary of Events and Information	Remarks and references to Appendices
FLESSELLES	1-2.16		The 59th continued their training from 1st – 5th March. On the 6-3-16 they marched via NAOURS – VALENCIENNES – CANDAS to HARDINVAL – road in fair order – very cold. Some snow showers	
HARDINVAL	6-3-16		Remained at HARDINVAL 7-8.6.16. Field some Musketry. On the 9-3-16 the 59th marched via OCCOCHES	
SERICOURT	9.3.16		BARLY – BONNIÈRES – FREVENT to SERICOURT. Road in fair order – very cold hard (ice). Snow by[?] about. The Division (including other divisions) taking over harassed line from NEUVILLE ST VAST to ROCLINCOURT (exclusive) from the 48 Regiment[?] (including) on the 9/10 completed on the 10-3-16. The 59th (from Guides) [for] reinforcements arriving in French on the 13/14. On the 10-3-16 the 59th (from Guides) [for] reinforcements arriving at Railhead (BOUQUEMAISON). Railhead moved to AUBIGNY on the 11-3-16. On the 11-3-8. N.C.O. + men went to WISQUES (training) + HORNHILL gas course of[?] (training) 18-3-16. On the 12-3-16 The	
BERLENCOURT	12-3-16		59th moved via FREVENT to BERLENCOURT. A first class road the greater part of the way in good order; Billets were dirty + bad. Horse lines in a filthy state. On the 14-3-16 the 59th	
TILLOY-LES-HERNAVILLE	14-3-16		marched via AMBRINES – CIR ERMONT – IZEL-LE-HAMEAU to TILLOY-LES HERNAVILLE. 2nd class road in good order – met 2 Batt[ery] (French) + Ambulance train (French) having lunch – fine + warm – billets were fair.	
VAUHECOURT	15-3-16		On the 15-3-16 the 59th marched via BERLES to HANDELICOURT – road in fair order. Open billets in huts, horses in open – fine + warm. On the 15-3-16 – 2 officers (Lt E J G Kirkpatrick + Lt H W Morland) with 50 O.R. marched via ETRUN to LOUEZ arriving at 7.30 P.M. – proceeded on foot to the trenches to be attached to 1/13 + 6th battalions, 1/4th Gordon Highlanders + take over T 8 – T 15 sectors. Sectors on the A.L. of L-154 Brigade French line.	

WAR DIARY
or
INTELLIGENCE SUMMARY.

Army Form C. 2118.

Place	Date	Hour	Summary of Events and Information	Remarks and references to Appendices
VANDELICOURT	1/3/16		These 2 troops were relieved with the 4th Gordons on the night of the 22/23 by the 4th SEAFORTHS. The GORDONS relieving troop billeted at ETRUN - the N.I.H. meeting their horses at LOUEZ on 12 m.d.s. relieved to VANDELICOURT. During the six days the N.I.H. were in the trenches, they had one casualty (Pte HARVEY). He was struck in the chest & eye by a fragment from a rifle grenade. There was a great deal of work for those in the trenches, to render them more secure & bullet proof - the trenches being much confused by the continuous fighting that had taken place on previous occasions when held by the French. The dug outs were deep & got our insufficient in number - on one occupied dugouts which had been constructed by the Germans. Captures by the French. The weather during the week was fine & warm, but cold at L-22°. - Snow fell on L-23° & 24° & the weather became wild & broken. 1 N.C.O. was sent on a course of instruction in GAS appliances permission on L-28° on the 3rd LEADAIR & troop proceeded to FALLIEVRE to be attached to the (?) Hauders (Indian Cav?) (in ?) on - Course of instruction. On the 20-2-16. Leave for the Division recovered & the 15th were permitted to draw 1 officer & 5 men every fortnight	

Army Form C. 2118.

"D" N.I.H₃₅ Vol.

WAR DIARY
or
INTELLIGENCE SUMMARY.

(Erase heading not required.)

WAR DIARY
of
D Sqⁿ NORTH IRISH HORSE

From April 1ˢᵗ 1916 to April 30ᵗʰ 1916

(VOLUME IV)

51

WAR DIARY or INTELLIGENCE SUMMARY

Army Form C. 2118.

Place	Date	Hour	Summary of Events and Information	Remarks and references to Appendices
VANDELICOURT	1-4-16		3 Troops of D Sqn N.I.H. & VANDELI COURT. 1 Troop under Lt ADAIR was attached to the 17 Lancers (Indian Cav Corps) at FILLIEVRE on the 31-3-16. All Divisional Mtd Troops (squadrons of SS N.I.H. - 1/SS Yorks Hussars - 46 Div & 1 SS Lothian Border Horse - 25 Div) - Cyclists Cos & Machine Gun Cos took part in a scheme under Inspector General of Cav & LtSH S-J. Brig. commanding XVII Corps on the 3 & 6 of this month. Capn V LOCKETT 17 Lancers was attached to this Corps HQ Staff as Umpire. The Troops to which was - Universal Method arrived at L'ECALON. Lt KIRK-PATRICK & 3 O.R. attended a HOTCHKISS GUN course at CAMIERS from 10-4-16 to 15-4-16. — Officers & NCOs attended an unsuccessful demonstration of Lewis gun fire (Flammenwerfer) on the 13-4-16. A party consisting of 20 men were brought to the King Edwards Horse French School at HESDIN from the 15-4-16 till the end of the month. Hotchkiss gun courses of 1 Officer & 6 N.C.O's when were trained for 5 days each course - at MURLAND. Lt P. SHERSTON being the Officer Instructor. Officers NCOs & men were instructed under Div A.P.M. in Military Police & road control duties. Each course lasts 15 days. HER MAJESTY QUEEN ALEXANDRA sent a number of gifts to the men of the Squadron on the 4-4-16. — The weather during the first 3 weeks of April was cold with a strong westerly wind blew daily — the last week the wind was fine - hot with light showers. — The battle of VERDUN starting on the 15th Feb 16 appears to have terminated about the 28-4-16. — The Sinn Fein rebellion started in DUBLIN on the 24-4-16 and is still continuing.	